SCIENTIFIC PATHWAYS

EVOLUTION

Investigating the Origin and Development of Species

JEN GREEN

New York

This edition first published in 2013 by:

The Rosen Publishing Group, Inc.
29 East 21st Street
New York, NY 10010

Consultant: Don Franceschetti, Ph.D., Distinguished Service Professor, Departments of Physics and Chemistry, The University of Memphis, Memphis, Tennessee

Creative Director: Jeni Child
Picture Researcher: Helen Simm
Illustrators: Darren Awuah, Richard Burgess, and Mark Walker
Managing Editor: Tim Harris
Children's Publisher: Anne O'Daly
Production Director: Alastair Gourlay
Editorial Director: Lindsey Lowe

Library of Congress Cataloging-in-Publication Data

Green, Jen.
Evolution: investigating the origin and development of the species/Jen Green.—1st ed.
p. cm.—(Scientific pathways)
Includes bibliographical references and index.
ISBN 978-1-4488-7198-8 (library binding)
1. Evolution (Biology)—Juvenile literature. I. Title.
QH367.1.G743 2013
576.8—dc23

2011044497

Manufactured in the United States of America

CPSIA Compliance Information: Batch #S12YA: For further information, contact Rosen Publishing, New York, New York, at 1-800-237-9932.

Every effort has been made to trace the owners of copyrighted material.

PHOTOGRAPHIC CREDITS

Cover: Shutterstock

AKG: Jean-Louis Nou 6; **Ardea:** Pat Morris 29, 35t, D. Parer & E. Parer-Cook 20, 21t; **Corbis:** Bettmann 14b, 15t, Layne Kennedy 7b, 8r, Kevin Schafer 1, Onne Van der Wal 17, Vo Trung Dung 16b; **Corel:** 13; **Getty Images:** Hulton Archive 10t, 22; **Nature Picture Library:** John Downer 25; **NHPA:** G. I. Bernard 23tl, Stephen Dalton 33bl, 33br, Ernie Janes 24, Roy Waller 36b; **NASA:** 8l; **National Library of Medicine:** 10b, 23tr; **Photodisc:** 4–5, 12, 15, 37; **Rex Features:** Jeremy Sutton Hibbert 35b, 36t; **Science Photo Library:** D. Van Ravensway 31, 32t; **Still Pictures:** Norbert Wu 32b; **Topham Picturepoint:** 7t, 11t, 11b, 14t, 16t, 18, 26, 27t, 27b; **University of Pennsylvania Library:** Smith Collection 28.

Illustrators: Darren Awuah, Richard Burgess, and Mark Walker

CONTENTS

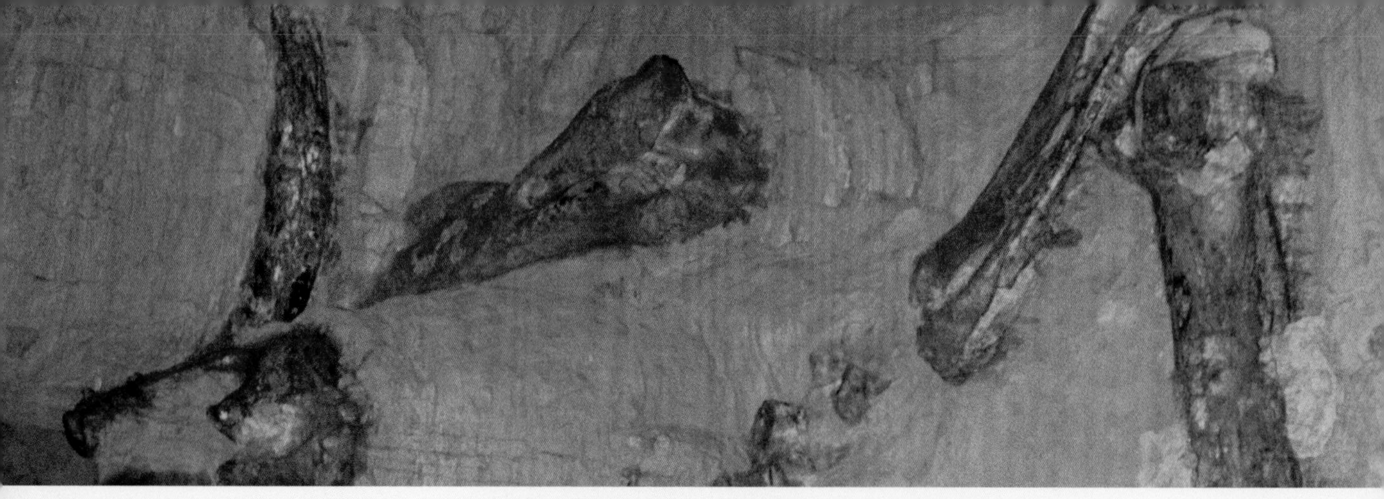

INTRODUCTION

Evolution is the process through which living things change with time and new species form. Evolution is central to modern biology and important in many other sciences, too. Yet it was shocking when it was first suggested in the 1850s, because it challenged the accepted view of how life began on Earth.

ENGLISH NATURALIST CHARLES Darwin (1809–1882) developed his theory of evolution after he sailed the world in a ship called HMS *Beagle*. Darwin kept his ideas secret for years. Eventually, he published a book known as *The Origin of Species* in 1859.

Darwin maintained that species (types of organisms) evolved through a process he called natural selection. Darwin realized that more young are born than can survive, which leads to a struggle to survive and breed. He also realized that successful individuals are likely to have more offspring than their rivals. The young inherit their parents' successful characteristics and have their own young. Over the generations, more and more individuals within a population will inherit the favored

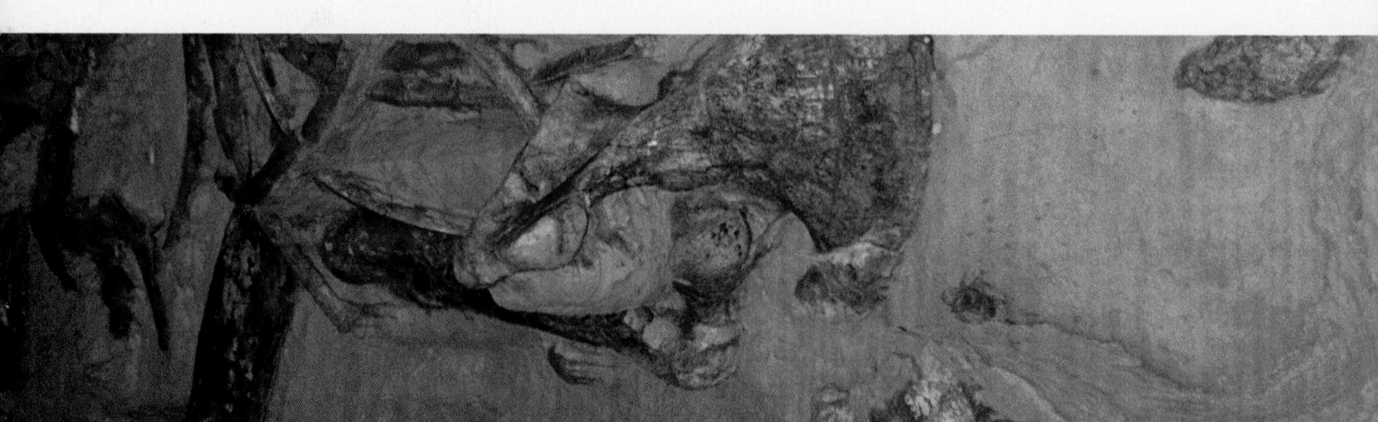

characteristics. Through this process, species change and new species evolve.

Fossils provide important evidence for the theory of evolution. They are the remains or traces of animals, plants, or other organisms that lived and died long ago. The fossil record shows that living things have existed on Earth for more than 3.5 billion years.

Life probably began in the oceans. Simple, bacteria-like life forms evolved over many years into more complex creatures. Over millions of years, all the types of living things we know today have evolved. Many thousands of others have died out. Only a fraction of Earth's species survive today.

The theory of evolution is backed up not only by fossils but also by other kinds of evidence. The distribution of modern species may give clues to their ancestors. Other clues may come from an animal's appearance. In the late twentieth century, scientists began to investigate DNA for chemical clues to evolution.

In the more than one hundred and fifty years since Darwin proposed his theory, scientists have found out much more about how evolution works. Evolution is hard to observe since it is slow, and scientists' quest to fully understand the process will continue for a long time.

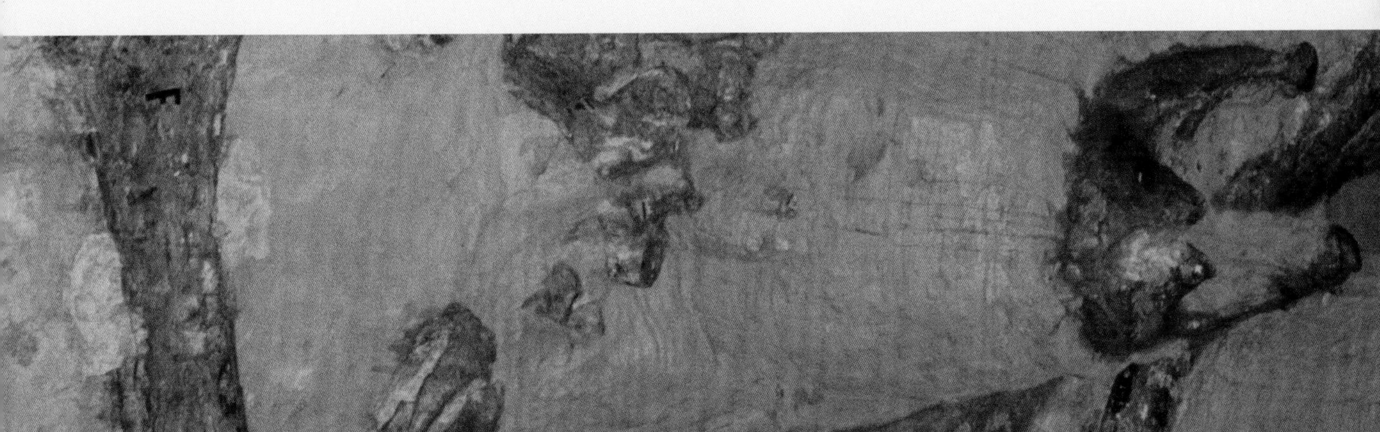

1 EARLY IDEAS

The mystery of how Earth and all the living things on it came into being has fascinated people for thousands of years. Around twenty-five hundred years ago, the Greeks started to investigate the forces that shaped Earth.

SINCE THE BEGINNING OF history, people have tried to find answers to the difficult questions of how Earth began and the origins of plants and animals. In ancient times, myths (traditional stories) to explain Earth's origins developed all around the world. Many of these stories, such as the Chinese creation story, featured a powerful supernatural

CHINESE CREATION STORY

A Chinese legend tells how, in the beginning, the universe was a confused, chaotic mass shaped like an enormous egg. A giant named Pan Ku emerged, took an ax, and split the egg-shaped mass in two. All the hot, bright, dry elements rose up to become the heavens, and all the cold, dark, moist elements sank down to form Earth. Later, when Pan Ku died, his body formed the mountains, rivers, and other natural features on Earth.

THE GREEK LEGEND OF CHAOS

The ancient Greeks believed that the universe began in a confused mass called Chaos. Slowly out of Chaos developed Gaia, or Mother Earth, along with the force of Love, which brings living things together so they can reproduce. Gaia eventually gave birth to Uranus, god of the night sky. These two united and produced the twelve Titans, who were the first living beings.

This wall painting from the first century CE shows Gaia surrounded by guardians.

THE GREAT FLOOD

The Old Testament story of the Flood tells how God decided to punish people's wickedness by drowning them in a flood. He instructed the one good man, Noah, to build a boat called an ark, and to take on board a pair of every animal. This picture (right) shows a medieval painting of the ark. After forty days and nights of rain, the whole Earth was flooded. When the flood dried up, Noah, his family, and the animals emerged from the ark to repopulate the purified Earth. Over the centuries, people have often used the story of the biblical flood to explain the existence of fossils or argue against evolution.

being or beings that created Earth and all living things. Other stories, such as the Greek legend of Chaos, described the world as gradually evolving from a misty nothingness.

The biblical account of Creation, which Jews, Christians, and Muslims share, appears in the first chapter of the Old Testament. It tells how God (or Allah) created Earth, the heavens, and all living things out of nothingness in the space of six days. Then God created humans in his image, and gave them the rest of creation to rule over. Later, people became wicked, and God sent The Great Flood to punish them.

EARTH'S SURFACE

In the sixth century BCE, the Greek thinker Anaximander (*c.* 610–546 BCE) suggested that water helped shape Earth's surface. Rivers, for example, deposit silt at their mouths and form deltas. In the first century BCE, Strabo (*c.* 64 BCE–23 CE) published a huge work on geography. He suggested that earthquakes and volcanic eruptions helped form the land.

This satellite picture shows mud deposits (pink) on the delta of the Mississippi River (red).

FOSSILS AND THE FLOOD

In medieval times, Christians believed that the Great Flood had transformed Earth's surface by shaping coastlines and depositing the rocks and sediment that form mountains and plains. People generally believed that Earth's surface had not changed since the time of the Flood. It was thought that fossils found high on mountains were the remains of drowned animals that were washed there by the waters of the Great Flood.

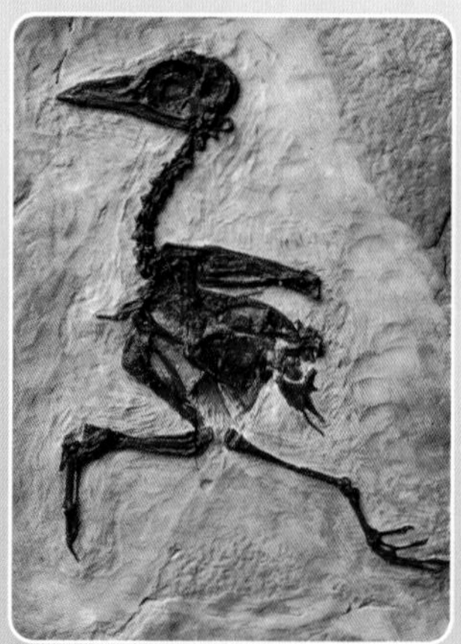

This fossil of a prehistoric bird was found in Wyoming.

The civilization of ancient Greece thrived from about 1000 to 200 BCE. The Greeks thought logically as they pondered the nature and origins of Earth. Most early people believed Earth was flat, but the Greeks used logic to figure out that it was round. Greek thinkers such as Anaximander and Strabo suggested that natural forces such as volcanoes, earthquakes, and rivers shaped Earth's surface.

People had long been puzzled by how fossils form and what they were. Prehistoric people collected fossils and sometimes wore them as jewelry.

They may have believed that fossils could work magic. The Greek thinker Pythagoras was among the first to guess that fossils were remains of once-living things that had turned to stone.

When the Romans conquered Greece around 250 BCE, they took over Greek learning and added to it. The Roman Empire itself fell in the fifth century CE. In the centuries that followed, much of the ancient learning was lost. Christianity spread through Europe at that time. Christians took the account of Creation and the Great Flood literally. They believed that God formed the world in six days. This version of Earth's origins prevailed for hundreds of years. It was difficult for people to argue against the views of the powerful Christian church.

HOW FOSSILS FORM

During the sixth century BCE, the philosopher Pythagoras (*c.* 569–475 BCE) suggested that fossils might be the remains of living things. In the fifth century BCE, the historian Herodotus (*c.* 485–425 BCE) noted that fossils of sea creatures were sometimes found in rocks high on mountains. He realized correctly that the rocks had once been underwater.

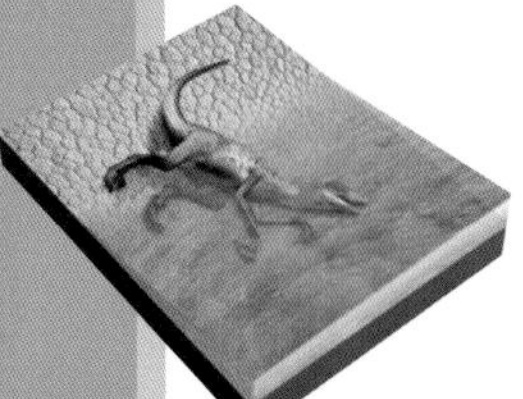

1. A dinosaur dies.

2. The body is quickly covered by layers of sediment, such as in a flash flood.

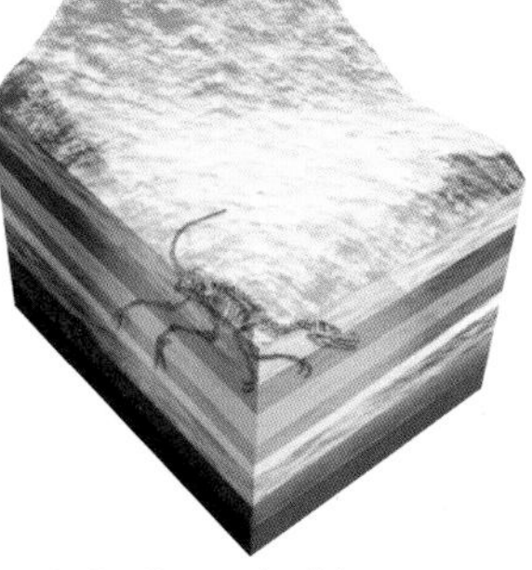

3. Sediment builds up over millions of years and hardens into rock.

4. Millions of years later, rain and wind wear the rock down and make the fossil visible to fossil hunters.

Many fossils occur in rocks made by layers of hardened silt and mud. An animal's bones decay slowly and are replaced by minerals in the rocks. This creates the fossils.

2 CREATION OR EVOLUTION?

After the Renaissance, Western thinkers began to study nature more scientifically, but everyone still believed the Bible's version of Creation. In the early nineteenth century, a French naturalist named Jean-Baptiste de Lamarck was among the first to publish an idea of evolution.

DURING THE FIFTEENTH AND sixteenth centuries, Christian thinkers continued to rely on the Bible to explain Earth's origins. In 1650, an Irish archbishop, James Ussher, studied the Old Testament and

DATING CREATION

Archbishop James Ussher (1581–1656; right) painstakingly added up the ages of people mentioned in the Old Testament to figure out the exact date of Creation: Sunday, October 23, 4004 BCE. This date was then printed in new copies of the Bible. It meant that Earth was less than six thousand years old. Using the same method, the bishop calculated that the Great Flood, or Deluge, had occurred in 2349 BCE.

BARON GEORGES CUVIER

Georges Cuvier (1769–1832; left) taught at the Museum of Natural History in Paris, one of the world's greatest scientific institutions. An expert on both fossils and anatomy, Cuvier had a reputation of being able to figure out what an extinct animal had looked like from just a few fossil bones. A devout Christian, he took the Bible's account of Creation as historical fact.

proposed exact dates for both the Creation and the Flood.

The seventeenth and eighteenth centuries saw the dawn of a new age of scientific enquiry called the Enlightenment. Scientists gradually discovered more about the forces that had shaped Earth. By the late eighteenth century, scientists—including a French naturalist called Baron Georges Cuvier—realized that fossils provided evidence of the events that had occurred in Earth's early history. After he studied rocks and fossils, Cuvier concluded that a series of natural catastrophes, including earthquakes and floods, had taken place in the distant past. Cuvier thought that the last of these disasters had been the biblical flood. According to the Bible, however, none of God's creatures had ever become extinct.

THE QUESTION OF EXTINCTION

The Bible story of the Flood did not mention extinction. It stated that two of every animal were taken aboard the ark. People thought that all species survived, and none was wiped out. In the late eighteenth century, the fossilized bones of huge creatures such as the giant sloth were discovered. At first people assumed that these animals were still alive in some remote corner of Earth. As more of the planet was explored, people realized more and more that the theory was unlikely. By the 1820s, most people accepted the idea of extinction. Devout Christians decided that some animals had missed the boat.

A reconstructed skeleton of Megatherium, *a giant sloth.*

LAMARCK'S IDEAS ON EVOLUTION

Lamarck believed that evolution happened as the muscles and other body parts of animals became stronger or weaker to suit their surroundings. For example, he thought giraffes evolved from shorter-necked beasts that had stretched their necks by reaching up to feed from trees. These animals then passed the long-necked characteristic on to their offspring. The idea that acquired (new) characteristics can be passed on in this way was later disproved.

LAMARCK VS. CUVIER

Baron Cuvier and Lamarck disagreed strongly about Earth's early history. The two scientists became enemies. Both were right in one way and wrong in another. Cuvier accepted the Bible story of Creation literally and so rejected the idea of evolution, but he accepted that some species had become extinct. Lamarck rejected both the Bible story and the idea of extinction. Lamarck believed that species did not become extinct, but evolved into new forms and so survived.

In 1809 the French naturalist Jean Baptiste de Lamarck (1744–1829) suggested his idea of evolution. Lamarck rightly suggested that species of living things changed over time. His mistake was to suggest something that scientists now think is impossible in nature. Lamarck's idea of evolution was that the bodies of individual animals changed during their lifetimes to suit their environment. Lamarck thought that animals passed on their newly acquired characteristics to their young.

Lamarck's theory was shocking at the time because it challenged the firmly held belief that God had created all animals in their present forms. Lamarck's ideas were rejected strongly by conventional Christians, including Baron Cuvier.

In the early nineteenth century, the fossilized remains of dinosaurs were unearthed. It became clear that many creatures that had existed in the past were no longer alive. People became keenly interested in Earth's early history, but the idea of evolution was still shocking for many people. At that time, a young man named Charles Darwin was growing up in England.

This drawing depicts Iguanodon, *the first species of dinosaur to be recognized from fossils.*

DINOSAUR DISCOVERIES

In 1822, English country doctor Gideon Mantell (1790–1852) and his wife Mary Ann found the fossilized teeth of a giant lizardlike creature in southern England. The Mantells named it *Iguanodon*, meaning "lizard-tooth." At first, no one took the Mantells' find seriously, but soon the bones of more giant reptiles came to light. In 1842, British scientist Richard Owen (1804–1892) coined the word *dinosaur*, meaning "terrible lizard," to describe these long-dead giants.

3 FINCHES AND TORTOISES

English naturalist Charles Darwin was not a promising student as a boy, but he came up with the world-changing theory of evolution after he sailed the world in the survey ship HMS *Beagle*.

CHARLES DARWIN WAS BORN IN 1809, in the small town of Shrewsbury, England. Young Charles did not enjoy school. He preferred the outdoor life and was a keen sportsman. He collected insects, rocks, shells, and birds' eggs. Darwin's father was a doctor, and he decided that Charles should become a doctor, too. Young Charles studied medicine at Edinburgh

STUDYING MEDICINE

In Darwin's day, there were no effective anesthetics, and medical operations were carried out on fully conscious patients. Darwin (left) was horrified by the sight of blood and the patients' screams. He abandoned the idea of being a doctor. Darwin's father doubted that his wayward son would ever do anything useful. He once told him: "You care for nothing but shooting, dogs, and rat-catching, and will be a disgrace to yourself."

HMS *BEAGLE*'S MISSION

The task of the *Beagle* crew was to sail around the world and map coastlines—in particular, the coastlines of South America and the Pacific islands. As they cruised offshore (right), the captain and a team of professional surveyors produced detailed charts that showed landmarks such as rocks and islands. They painstakingly measured the depth of coastal waters using a weighted line lowered from the ship.

University for two years but then gave up. He then went to Cambridge University, England, to study to become a clergyman.

At Cambridge, Darwin was interested in botany (plant studies) and geology (the study of rocks and fossils). He made friends with botany professor John Henslow (1796–1861). Soon after Darwin graduated as a young clergyman, Henslow learned that a survey ship named HMS *Beagle* was about to set sail on a world voyage. Henslow suggested Darwin join as a gentleman (unpaid) naturalist. The ship already had a paid expedition naturalist. Once he was accepted, Darwin packed the equipment he would need on the long voyage, including walking shoes, a microscope, and pistols to shoot specimens. He also took along a new book called *Principles of Geology* by the scientist Charles Lyell.

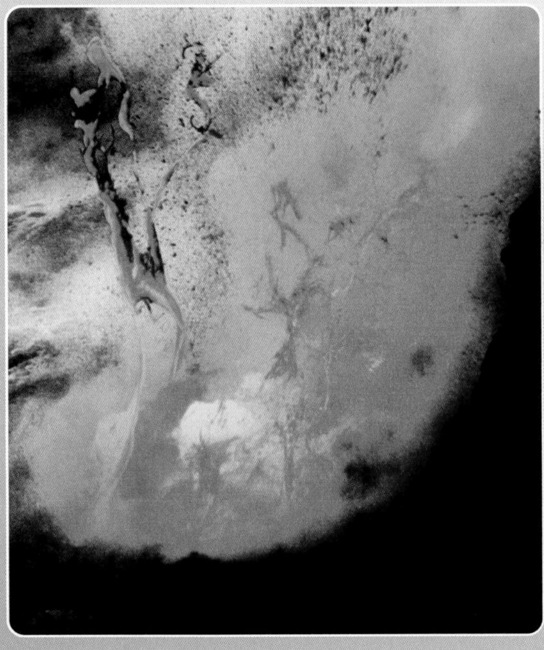

CHARLES LYELL

Charles Lyell (1797–1875) was one of a new generation of scientists who overturned traditional ideas about the age and origins of Earth. His book *Principles of Geology* was published in 1830, the year before Darwin sailed on the *Beagle*. Lyell proposed that Earth was much older than church leaders suggested—millions of years old, not thousands. He argued that the land was shaped continually by powerful natural forces such as volcanoes (left) and rivers. Darwin read *Principles of Geology* and was impressed by Lyell's ideas.

CAPTAIN FITZROY

At age 26, the *Beagle*'s captain, Robert Fitzroy (1805–1865; right), was not much older than Darwin. He was, however, already an experienced seaman and expert navigator, skilled at making charts. A devout Christian, Fitzroy believed that the Bible stories of Creation and the Flood were literally true. Darwin's more open-minded attitudes, inspired by new thinkers such as Charles Lyell, eventually caused conflict between the two men.

HMS *Beagle* set sail across the Atlantic from Plymouth, England, on December 26, 1831. Darwin was just twenty-two. As well as pursuing his own interests as a naturalist, Darwin was companion to the ship's captain, Robert Fitzroy. Darwin suffered badly from seasickness and spent much of the nine-week crossing in his cabin. When the ship reached South America, its naturalist left the expedition. Darwin took on the role and explored the Brazilian rain forest. He delighted in the lush plant life and multitude of unfamiliar mammals, insects, and birds.

As the *Beagle* cruised slowly down the South American coast, Darwin had plenty of time to carry out his work. He sometimes spent weeks ashore, where he traveled on horseback and

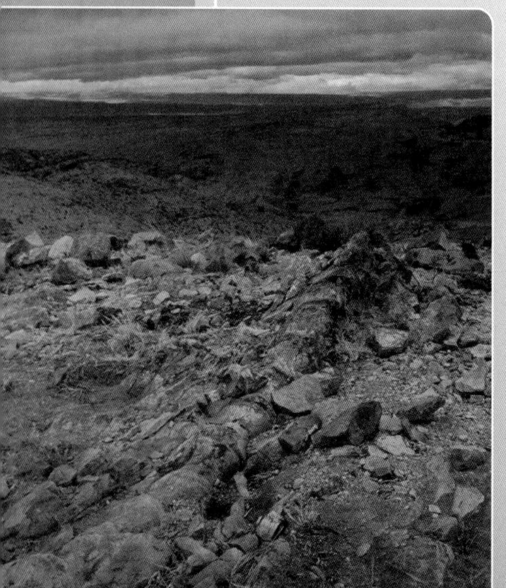

GIANT FOSSILS

At Punta Alta (left), a fossil site in Argentina, Darwin saw the remains of an extinct giant sloth and *Scelidotherium*, a huge beast that looked like a cross between an enormous anteater and an armadillo. He also saw the smaller, living relatives of these mammals. The fossils puzzled Darwin. He wondered what had caused the huge creatures to become extinct while their smaller cousins lived on. The Bible taught that it was the Great Flood. Darwin suspected that some other factor might have been responsible.

A CHILEAN EARTHQUAKE

When Darwin found fossilized seashells in the mountains, he marveled to discover them at such a height and so far from the sea. An earthquake Darwin witnessed on the coast of Chile provided him with a possible explanation. The quake raised the level of rocks on the shore by more than 3 feet (1 m). Over millions of years, this process, called uplift, could have raised rocks from the sea bed to form mountains. This was another clue that the accepted reading of the Bible, which stated that Earth was only a few thousand years old, might be wrong.

An earthquake in Chile (left) gave Darwin an insight into how mountains form.

investigated local geology and wildlife, before he rejoined the ship.

In Argentina, Darwin visited a site rich in giant fossils of huge extinct mammals, such as the giant sloth, *Megatherium* (see page 11). After the *Beagle* rounded the tip of South America, Darwin witnessed another amazing sight, an earthquake on the coast of Chile. The upheaval caused by the earthquake led Darwin to question traditional ideas about the age of Earth.

As it sailed northward, the *Beagle* visited the remote Galápagos Islands, which lie 800 miles (1,300 km) off the coast of Ecuador. These small, volcanic islands looked bleak and boring at first, but they held vital clues that would help Darwin formulate his theory of evolution. Darwin saw

COLLECTING FINCHES

Darwin found several different types of finches on the Galápagos. The birds of each species looked very similar in plumage but they had differently shaped beaks. Some of the little birds had stout beaks, useful for cracking seeds; others had slender beaks more suited to catching insects. The variety of bill sizes was so great that at first Darwin did not even realize the birds were all finches.

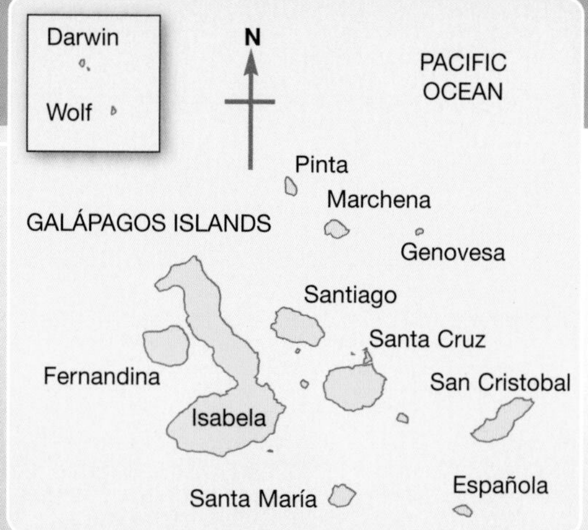

The Galápagos Islands are home to thirteen species of finches; Darwin saw six of them. The inset shows islands farther away.

TORTOISES OF THE GALÁPAGOS

The giant tortoises (right) of the Galápagos fascinated Darwin, especially when he learned that tortoises on different islands had different markings and differently shaped shells. The vice governor of the islands told him that he could tell which island a tortoise came from just by looking at it. This set Darwin thinking. He wondered if all the giant tortoises shared just one ancestor whose descendants changed in appearance over generations on each island.

that the Galápagos was home to plants and animals not found on the mainland of South America, including marine iguanas (lizards), finches (birds), and giant tortoises. The tortoises weighed up to 330 pounds (150 kg). Many of the small islands had their own species of animals found nowhere else.

After a month the *Beagle* sailed on across the Pacific. The crew visited Australia, New Zealand, and many of the Pacific islands. As in the Galápagos, Darwin found many of the islands held types of plants and animals that lived nowhere else. The voyage of the *Beagle* lasted five years. Finally, the ship sailed for home. Darwin reached England on October 27, 1836. He was now a wiser and more knowledgeable man and an experienced naturalist. Even so, he struggled to find answers to all the questions that his experiences on the voyage had raised. Darwin started to write about his experiences.

THE VOYAGE OF THE *BEAGLE*

The *Beagle* covered a total of 60,000 miles (96,000 km) on its historic voyage between 1831 and 1836. The main map (right) shows its route in red around South America. The full voyage is shown on the smaller map. The vessel was a three-masted sailing ship. It carried a crew of seventy men, including a team of surveyors, Darwin, the ship's naturalist, and an artist. The little boat measured just 100 feet (30 m) from prow to stern. Conditions on board were cramped.

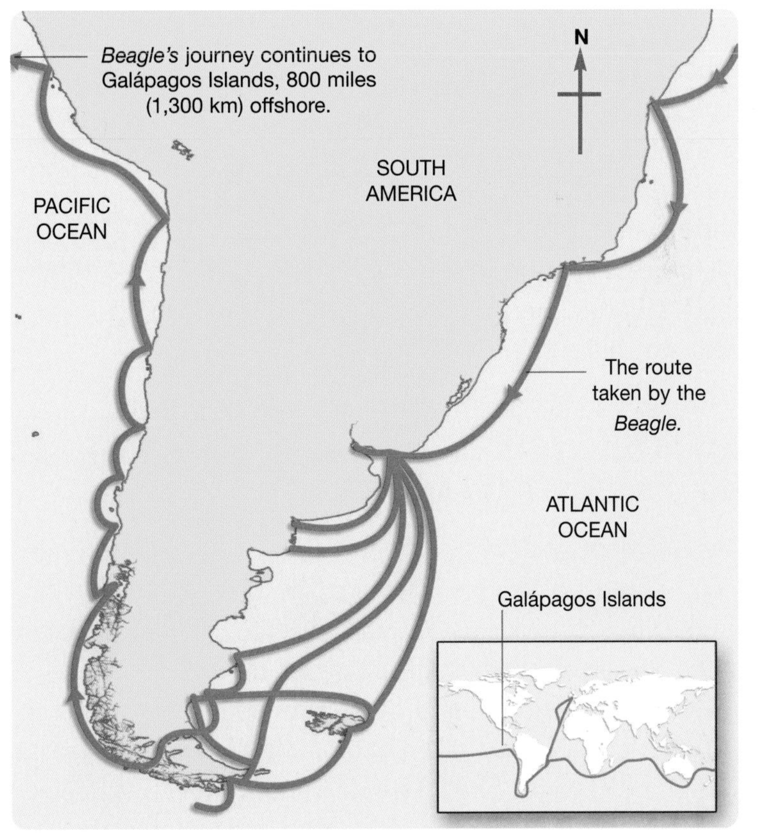

NATURAL SELECTION

The years that followed Darwin's return were a busy time for him. He wrote about his travels, got married, and began to formulate his theory of natural selection.

DARWIN RETURNED FROM THE *Beagle* to find he was already famous. Throughout the voyage he had sent specimens and long letters to his friend, the botanist John Henslow. Henslow had passed news of Darwin's discoveries to other scientists,

CORAL REEFS

In 1842, Darwin published a book about coral reefs. He presented his ideas about how ring-shaped islands of coral called atolls formed in tropical oceans. Darwin saw that corals formed reefs around volcanic islands. If these islands sank below the water, the corals would continue to grow and form a hollow ring of coral reef. This process would take thousands of years to create an atoll. Here was further proof that Earth was older than the church suggested.

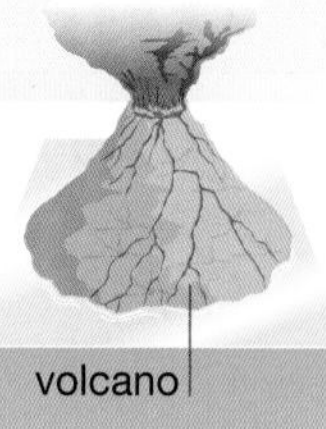

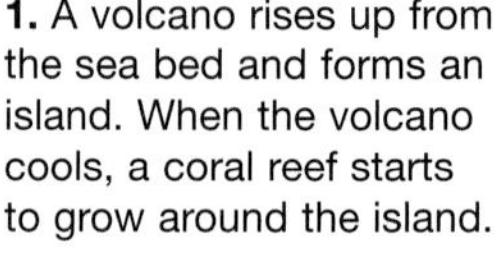

1. A volcano rises up from the sea bed and forms an island. When the volcano cools, a coral reef starts to grow around the island.

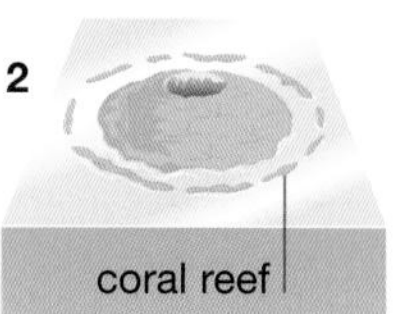

2. The island sinks below the waves again—perhaps because of a rise in sea level—but the coral continues to grow.

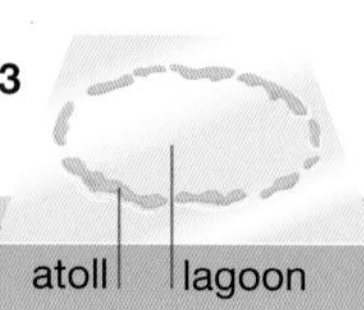

3. The island eventually disappears, which leaves the continually growing ring of reef, or atoll, surrounding an

GALÁPAGOS FINCHES

The existence of several different types of finches on one group of islands troubled Darwin. The birds looked very similar in most respects but had different bill sizes. Darwin said: "Seeing this...diversity in structure in one small, intimately related group of birds, one might fancy that... one species had been taken and modified." He had guessed that the Galápagos birds were descended from one species yet had somehow changed. This idea contradicted the biblical Creation story, which stated that God had created all species of animals, once and for all, "in the beginning."

The cactus finch uses cactus spines as tools to capture insect grubs.

including Charles Lyell. Two important British scientific organizations, the Geological Society and the Royal Society, made Darwin a member. He moved to London to continue his work.

Toward the end of the voyage, Darwin had become interested in coral reefs. He published a book about them, together with a journal of his travels and a five-volume study of the wildlife he had seen. A bird expert examined Darwin's collection of finch specimens. He concluded that the small birds Darwin had collected on Galápagos were, despite their differing structures, all related types of finches.

Darwin felt increasingly lonely and, in 1839, he married his cousin, Emma Wedgwood. Soon after, he began to suffer from a mysterious illness.

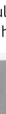

DARWIN'S ILLNESS

Darwin suffered from a mysterious illness that has never been identified. He went from being a strong, energetic young man to being weak and easily tired. Some experts think he caught a serious illness named Chagas disease, which is carried by the kissing bug (left), a biting insect. Darwin said he was bitten by one in South America. Other people believe that growing worries about how his new evolutionary ideas would be received by others may have brought on Darwin's illness.

Darwin's poor health continued, and he and Emma decided to move to the quiet village of Downe, south of London. They started a family and eventually had ten children. Darwin became more and more troubled by his growing belief that species of living things evolved, or gradually changed. The idea contradicted not only the accepted view of the Bible at that time but also the world of science. Darwin worried that if he published his ideas, his quiet life would end, all his scientist friends would reject him, and he would face severe criticism from strangers.

Darwin wrote to plant and animal breeders about selective breeding and started to breed pigeons himself.

SELECTIVE BREEDING

Darwin knew that breeders developed new strains of plants and animals by choosing favored specimens to breed from. The breeders knew that the next generation were likely to inherit features from their parents. For example, farmers mated their best cows with prize bulls (below) to get the most milk or meat from the calves. The process of improving livestock and crops by choosing their mates is called selective breeding. Darwin later called it artificial selection. He realized that selective breeding in the farmyard worked on similar principles to his theory of natural selection in the wild.

BREEDING PIGEONS

Darwin saw that pigeonkeepers developed new and unusual strains of birds (below). They bred pigeons with natural variations such as long feathers or short beaks. Darwin theorized that if people could cause so much change in a few generations by selective breeding, new species could evolve in the wild over many thousands of generations.

THOMAS MALTHUS

Economist Thomas Malthus (1766–1834; below) wrote about the growth of human populations. He stated that the human population would naturally double in as little as twenty-five years if not checked by war, hunger, and disease. As the number of people grew, food would become scarce. People would compete with one another for survival. Darwin realized that Malthus's words applied to the whole natural world, and not just to people. Food was always limited in the wild, so all living things took part in a struggle for survival, which is won by the strongest.

Darwin kept a secret notebook in which he recorded examples of variation and change in plant and animal species. In his mind, he went over and over his experiences on the *Beagle*. Darwin had become an evolutionist (someone who believes in evolution), but he could not figure out how evolution happened. Then Darwin came across a book by the economist Thomas Malthus. This provided the key to Darwin's understanding of evolution. Malthus suggested that life was a harsh struggle in which living things competed for survival. "Now I have a theory," Darwin wrote in his secret notebook.

NATURAL SELECTION

Darwin noticed that in nature, many more young were produced than could survive. If a pair of birds produced ten or more young each year (right), they could not all survive to breed themselves. This caused competition, or a struggle for existence, as the birds competed for limited resources. Darwin realized that variations between individuals would make each one either more or less suited to survive than the others. The most successful individuals would survive longer and produce more young. Darwin called them selected individuals. They would pass on their desirable characteristics to their offspring. Over generations, selected individuals would increase and out-compete the rest. Darwin called the process natural selection. Over time, natural selection would mold whole new species of animals and plants.

Darwin spent the next fourteen years in Downe, where he continued to develop his theory of natural selection. He gathered evidence from plant and animal breeders, biologists, and geologists in support of his ideas. Some people now think that collecting more and more information was Darwin's way of delaying writing his book about evolution for fear of the storm of protest it would surely cause.

On the outside, Darwin's life was calm and peaceful. He studied at home, went for walks, worked in the garden, and played with his children. On the inside, however, Darwin was terrified by what might happen if his views on evolution became known. He told a few friends about his ideas and said it was "like confessing a murder." Darwin put his work on evolution aside and studied small sea creatures called barnacles for the next eight years.

Then, one morning in 1858, he received a letter from a young scientist named Alfred Russel Wallace, who was working in Southeast Asia. Wallace's letter was a bombshell. It showed Darwin that his terrible secret could remain hidden no longer. Wallace had come up with exactly the same theory as Darwin.

ALFRED RUSSEL WALLACE

British naturalist Alfred Russel Wallace (1823–1913) came up with the idea of evolution while suffering from a serious illness, malaria, in Southeast Asia. The theory came to him as he lay on his sickbed in a fever. When Wallace recovered, he wrote to Darwin about it simply because Darwin was a well-known scientist. Wallace had no idea that Darwin had been at work on the same idea for the last twenty years.

Wallace's flying frog was named in honor of scientist Alfred Russel Wallace.

5 HOW NEW SPECIES EVOLVE

Wallace's letter shocked Darwin into publishing his theory of evolution. As he had feared, the book raised a storm of protest.

WHEN DARWIN TOLD HIS CLOSE friends about Wallace's letter, they advised him to publish his own ideas as soon as possible. Later that same year, essays by Darwin and Wallace about natural selection were read at a scientific meeting in London. Meanwhile, Darwin was struggling to condense the results of twenty years' work into a short book. *On the Origin of Species by Means of Natural Selection* was published on November 24, 1859. It

SURVIVAL OF THE FITTEST

Many of the phrases people most commonly associate with the book *On the Origin of Species by Means of Natural Selection* have little to do with Darwin. In his book, Darwin explained how species change by the process of natural selection. He did not even use the word evolution in his book. Nor did Darwin invent the phrase "survival of the fittest." That was coined by English philosopher Herbert Spencer in support of his theories on human nature. Spencer was inspired in his own work by Darwin's ideas on evolution.

A pair of finches from "The Zoology of the Voyage of HMS *Beagle,*" *1841*

INSPIRED BY THE *BEAGLE*

Darwin's book began: "When on board HMS *Beagle* as naturalist, I was much struck with certain facts." In the book, Darwin went on to use many examples from the voyage to support his theory of natural selection. Elsewhere, Darwin wrote: "The voyage of the *Beagle* has been by far the most important event in my life, and has determined my whole career."

THE DESCENT OF MAN

People often think that Darwin wrote about human evolution in *Origin*. It was in a later book, *The Descent of Man*, published in 1871, that Darwin said that people and apes were descended from a common ancestor. *The Descent of Man* caused a commotion. Many people misunderstood what Darwin was saying about human evolution. Cartoons like this one (left) suggested that Darwin believed humans were descended from monkeys. In fact, he thought that although apes and humans shared a common mammal ancestor, both had since continued to evolve.

sold out immediately. Other authors invented phrases such as "survival of the fittest" to sum up Darwin's theory.

Darwin's book drew on ideas from biology, geology, and the study of fossils. Above all, he was inspired by his experiences on the *Beagle*. Darwin maintained that all species on Earth had evolved from a few common ancestors, which were perhaps themselves descended from just one simple form of life.

In a later book, *The Descent of Man*, Darwin applied his theory of natural selection to human evolution. This contradicted the church's accepted view that people were different from animals because they were made "in God's likeness." Darwin believed that humans and apes evolved from

HENRY HUXLEY

Henry Huxley (1825–1895; right) read Darwin's book and was convinced right away. He wrote: "My reflection [when I first made myself master of the central idea] was . . . how extremely stupid not to have thought of that!" Huxley became a firm supporter of Darwin and earned the nickname "Darwin's bulldog."

the same apelike ancestors. As Darwin had long expected, his work inspired strong feelings. A few scientists, particularly the biologist Henry Huxley, were won over immediately. Other scientists and churchmen, however, were shocked.

In 1860, an important debate about evolution took place at Oxford University, England. The church and Darwin's supporters met head-on. The famous speaker Bishop Samuel Wilberforce (1805–1873) presented the traditional Christian view. Henry Huxley spoke for Darwin, because Darwin himself was too ill to go. Wilberforce ridiculed Darwin's ideas passionately. Then Huxley spoke with clear logic in support for Darwin's ideas. Huxley won the

QUICK ACCEPTANCE

Despite the controversy that followed Darwin's books, his ideas were accepted surprisingly quickly. Natural selection provided a scientific explanation for the fossils of dinosaurs and other extinct creatures. Evolution also fitted with the popular idea of human progress, which was fashionable at the time. The idea that people were special because God made them that way was replaced by the idea of humans as the superior end product of evolution. Scientists now think of evolution as a continuing process, not a route to an end product.

debate, and the meeting ended in pandemonium.

After the Oxford triumph, more scientists were converted to the idea of evolution. Over the next twenty years, Darwin's ideas were met with quick acceptance, not just in Britain but also in Europe and America. The discovery of an amazing new fossil called *Archaeopteryx* helped. Meanwhile, Darwin continued to work quietly from home. He published several books about natural selection. By the time of Darwin's death at the age of seventy-three, his views were accepted widely. As a mark of respect, the scientist was buried in London's great church, Westminster Abbey. In the space of just a few years, the *Beagle*'s amateur naturalist had transformed people's ideas about the history of life on Earth.

ARCHAEOPTERYX

In 1861, just a few years after *Origin* was published, a remarkable fossil came to light in a quarry in Germany. The fossil was named *Archaeopteryx*. The discovery supported Darwin's idea that all species were descended from just a few ancestors. *Archaeopteryx* appeared to be a halfway stage between reptiles and birds. It had the claws, teeth, and bony tail of a reptile, but the feathers of a bird. *Archaeopteryx* provided evidence that birds evolved from reptiles, an idea that scientists now accept.

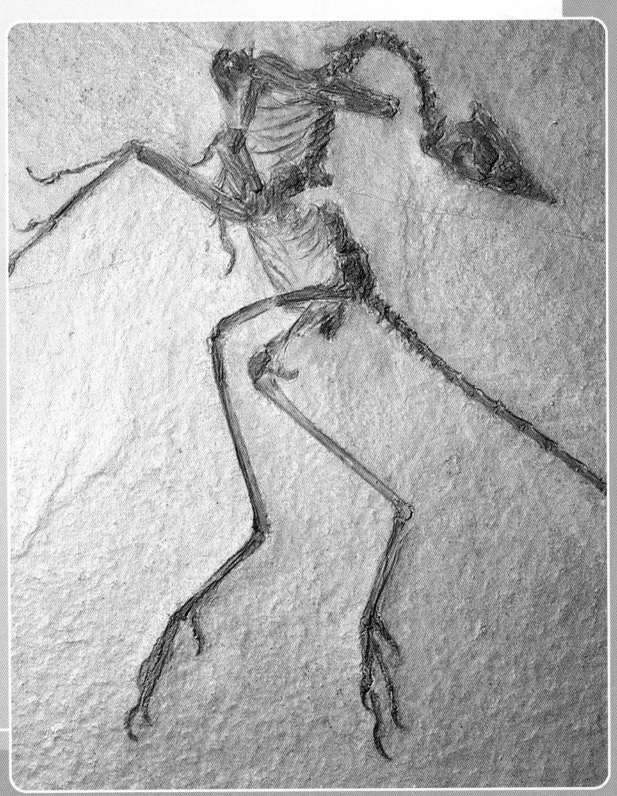

This fossil of Archaeopteryx *is around 150 million years old.*

6 GENES, HEREDITY, AND MUTATION

By 1900, most scientists had accepted the principle of evolution but did not know how characteristics were passed from one generation to the next. Part of the question had been answered years before by an Austrian monk.

AROUND 1900, SCIENTISTS BEGAN to understand the principles of genetics (inheritance). Part of the answer lay unnoticed in the forgotten work of an Austrian monk named Gregor Mendel (1822–1884), who had experimented on peas in his monastery garden in the 1850s. Mendel's discovery was that heredity followed simple mathematical rules. In 1866 he published his results.

MENDEL'S DISCOVERY

Mendel bred varieties of pea that produced seeds of two different colors, yellow and green. He observed that some inherited characteristics (features) were common, including yellow seeds, while others were rare, including green seeds. When Mendel crossed peas that produced only yellow seeds with those that produced only green seeds, all the offspring were yellow. This is because each offspring inherited two forms, or alleles, of the gene for seed color from the parents: a dominant yellow allele from one parent and a recessive green allele from the other. The dominant allele had masked the recessive one, producing yellow seeds. For a plant to produce green seeds, it needs two recessive alleles. This could only happen in the second generation. When Mendel crossed two first-generation offspring, the second generation produced mainly yellow seeds and a few green ones, always in a three to one ratio.

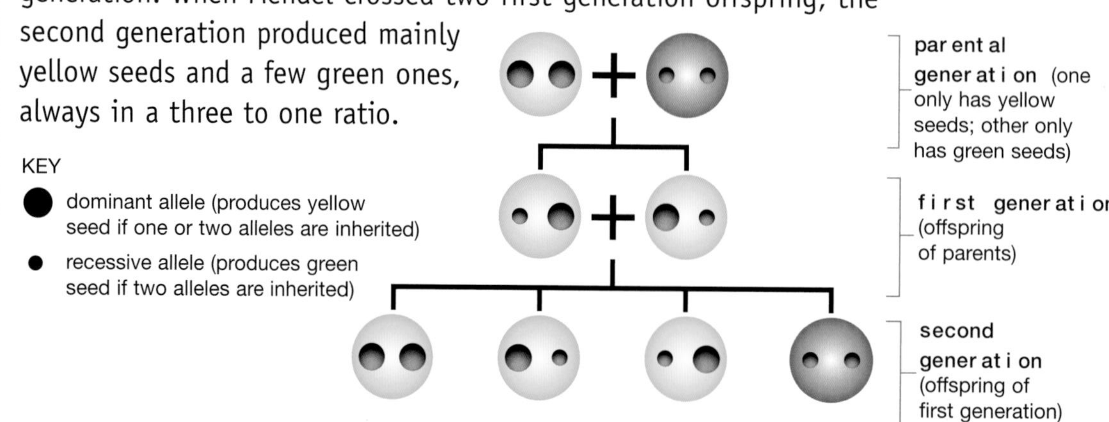

HOW NEW SPECIES EVOLVE

Darwin called the puzzle of how new species arise (speciation) the "mystery of mysteries." Scientists now know of a number of ways that speciation occurs. One way it can happen is if different populations of a single species become separated. An example is when birds settle on an isolated island. If environmental conditions are different for each of the populations, natural selection may mold them in different ways. The two populations may eventually form different species. Evolution is a continual process, so it is not always possible to say exactly when a new species arises. Speciation may be quick or may take millions of years.

MUTATION

When a cell divides or replicates (copies itself; below), its genes also copy themselves. The new cells each carry a copy. Just as mistakes can occur when people copy writing or a computer program, random mistakes arise when genes are copied in cells. Such mistakes are called mutations. Some mutations are passed on to the next generation. If a mutated gene benefits the young, they are more likely to succeed in breeding, and the mutation may spread in a population. Mutation is one of the things that causes genetic variation. Natural selection acts on genetic variation.

Mendel suggested that "hereditary particules," which we now call genes, carried inheritable characteristics. No one understood the significance of Mendel's work until twentieth-century scientists produced similar results. Then people realized Mendel was first.

In 1910 American zoologist Thomas Hunt Morgan (1866–1945) tried to disprove Mendel's ideas but ended up supporting them. Morgan bred fruit flies with features such as eyes or wings of a particular color. Fruit flies breed quickly and frequently produce random variations called mutations. Morgan not only got results similar to Mendel's but also found out why. Threadlike structures called chromosomes in the flies' cells carried genes that contained the instructions that controlled heredity. Morgan's work helped to explain how new species evolve.

COELACANTH: A "LIVING FOSSIL"

Millions of years ago, before animals with backbones had moved onto the land from the oceans, a group of fish with muscular, fleshy fins evolved. Scientists think that descendants of these lobe-finned fish, or perhaps an unknown but similar group of fish, evolved limbs and walked on land. In 1938, a freshly dead coelacanth (below) was discovered in South Africa. Scientists thought at first it must be a hoax or a mistake. They believed that lobe-finned fish such as the coelacanth had been extinct for millions of years. Since then, a second species of coelacanth has been discovered living in the Indian Ocean.

MASS EXTINCTIONS

Charles Darwin wrote: "No fact in the long history of the world is so startling as the wide and repeated exterminations of its inhabitants." Scientists gradually assembled evidence of several mass extinctions that had wiped out huge numbers of species at once. At least five major extinctions occurred in prehistory. The last, which struck sixty-five million years ago, wiped out the dinosaurs. Mass extinctions may be caused by natural disasters such as wide-scale volcanic eruptions, rapid climate change, or even by meteorites striking Earth (above).

Morgan's work was followed up in the 1930s and 1940s by Ukrainian American geneticist Theodosius Dobzhansky (1900–1975). Dobzhansky also bred fruit flies. Dobzhansky and others—including German-born zoologist Ernst Mayer and British biologist Julian Huxley (1887–1975), grandson of Darwin's friend, Henry Huxley—developed the synthetic theory of evolution. This theory combined, or synthesized, Darwin's ideas with the newly discovered principles of genetics.

The discovery of new fossils helped scientists continue to piece together the puzzle of evolutionary history. Some of the fossils seemed to represent intermediate stages between species, or even between whole different groups of animals, such as reptiles and birds. Living links between fossil species and species alive today were discovered, including the coelacanth. The fossil record also provided evidence of mass extinctions, when many species died out at once. Living species, including Darwin's finches, continue to show the process of evolution in action.

EVOLUTION IN ACTION

In the early nineteenth century, most peppered moths had light-colored wings (below left; lower). A rare variation produced a few with dark wings (below left; upper). When trees became blackened by soot from factories, dark peppered moths were better camouflaged than pale ones (below right). Dark moths almost entirely replaced pale ones in towns. Another example of evolution in action came from Darwin's finches. Scientists measured the bills of one species over several years. They found that when food was scarce, big-billed finches became more common. One of Darwin's inspirations had helped demonstrate his theory at work.

7 FUTURE PROSPECTS

The theory of natural selection has hardly changed since Darwin's time, but scientists have since learned more about how evolution works. Whole new branches of science have developed from our modern understanding of evolution and heredity.

DURING THE 1940S, SCIENTISTS identified deoxyribonucleic acid (DNA), a chemical found in the chromosomes inside cells, as the messenger substance that transmits characteristics from parents to young. Each molecule of DNA contains a set of coded instructions that control

THE STRUCTURE OF DNA

In 1953, Francis Crick (born 1916) and James Watson (born 1928) figured out that the structure of DNA was a double helix, a shape like a twisted ladder (right). The rungs of the ladder are formed by combinations of just four chemical compounds, called bases. The four bases fit together only in pairs. DNA copies itself by splitting in two. Every base on each strand attracts a new base of its opposite type. The process is complete when an exact copy of the original double helix is made. By copying itself exactly, DNA carries the code to the next generation. Mistakes in the copying process cause mutations, one of the causes of the variation that drives natural selection.

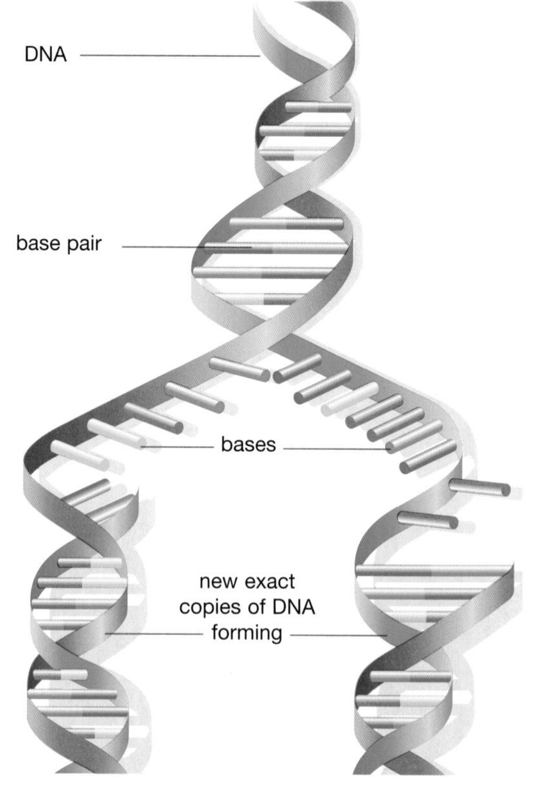

Did animals such as this aardvark evolve gradually or in a rapid burst?

THE RATE OF EVOLUTIONARY CHANGE

The theory of evolution by natural selection is a simple one, but determining how evolution works in nature is more complex. Evolutionary scientists argue about subtle differences between theories. One continuing argument is over the rate of evolutionary change. Supporters of gradualism think that evolution is a gradual process that happens slowly over millions of years. Supporters of punctuated equilibrium argue that periods of rapid change occur when a population becomes isolated from others of its species or when major environmental changes occur. The bursts of evolutionary action are sandwiched between long periods in which little happens. Both theories have many supporters.

heredity. In the 1950s, scientists Francis Crick and James Watson figured out the structure of DNA. Scientists could at last understand how characteristics are passed from parents to their young.

Evolutionists continued to argue, however, about the rate of evolutionary change. Scientists traditionally thought natural selection molded species at a steady rate over millions of years. This theory is called gradualism. However, in the 1970s, Stephen Jay Gould (1941–2002) suggested an alternative theory called punctuated equilibrium. This states that evolutionary change happens in bursts. Arguments also centered around whether evolution acts on species, populations and groups, and individuals, or just on their DNA.

CLONES

A clone is a genetically identical copy of a living thing. Plants reproduce by cloning when they grow from cuttings instead of seeds. Identical twins are clones. Scientists are now learning how to make clones artificially from cells of adult animals. In 1997, Scottish scientists cloned a sheep named Dolly (right). Some people fear that the same techniques will be used to clone humans.

In 1976 Richard Dawkins (born 1941) published a book called *The Selfish Gene*. He suggested that natural selection acted on DNA itself, not the animal or plant that carries the genes. To Dawkins, animals and plants were like machines that carried DNA. If a gene helped an animal survive and reproduce, the gene was passed to the next generation and became more common.

In the 1970s and 1980s, discoveries about genetics (the study of heredity and mutation) led to the development of the new science of genetic engineering. Scientists discovered how to insert new genes into DNA in the

THE GENOME

Animal and plant cells contain DNA. The DNA carries all the genes needed to make an organism. An entire set of genes is called a genome. In the 1990s, scientists started to translate the genetic code. The sea squirt (left) genome was one of the first they understood completely. By 2011 geneticists had almost completed the map of the human genome; those for other living things were being studied. The maps will show where each gene is and what it does. They may help doctors find cures for genetic diseases.

laboratory, to alter characteristics of living species. Genetic engineering techniques are now used to produce new food crops, medicines, and even clones (exact copies) of animals.

Scientists are now mapping the entire genetic material, or genome, of many animals and plants. They hope to learn how all genes affect living things.

The study of evolution has spawned whole sciences, such as genetics, and strongly influenced many others, including ecology. These new sciences have changed the way people look at the world. Were it not for Darwin's theory of evolution by natural selection, scientists would have a much poorer understanding of the world around us.

ECOLOGY

Ecology is the study of interrelationships between living things and their environment. This branch of biology started in the twentieth century. Before then, biologists mostly collected animals and plants from the wild and studied them in a laboratory. When biologists began to study ecology, they realized the need to view living things in their natural homes. For example, African elephants need to be studied in an African savanna (below). The science of ecology has also made people more aware of their own position in the natural world and how human activities affect the whole planet.

EARTHWORM HABITAT

GOALS

1. Create a miniature earthworm habitat.

2. Observe the interactions of organisms and their environment.

WHAT YOU WILL NEED

- clear container, such as a fishbowl or a plastic cup
- gravel
- sand
- potting soil
- compost
- chopped-up plant material
- straw
- spray bottle filled with water
- earthworms
- black paper
- tape

1 Into the container place a layer of gravel 1 inch (2.5cm) deep. Top with ½ inch (1cm) of potting soil, then 1 inch (2.5cm) of sand, 1 inch (2.5cm) of compost, and another ½ inch (1cm) of sand.

2 Top with chopped-up leaves, straw, and dead plant material.

3 Spray each layer with the water bottle as you put it in.

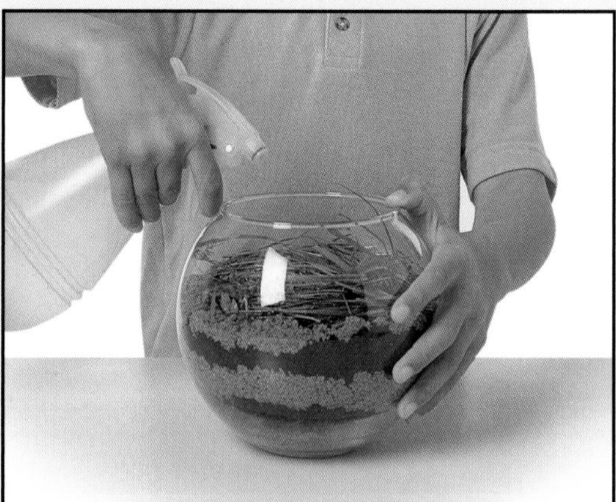

DARWIN'S EARTHWORMS

Charles Darwin, the pioneer of evolution, spent more time studying earthworms than any other kind of organism.

4 Place the earthworms on top of the material in the container.

5 Cut out a circle of black paper to fit over the top of the container. Tape it in place, and make pinholes in the lid to allow air in.

TROUBLESHOOTING

What if my earthworms start to die?

Remember to keep the contents of the bowl moist. If you are using a large bowl, then you can house more than one earthworm. Dig the earthworms out of your backyard or buy them at most pet stores. Remember, worms are living creatures, and you should try not to hurt them in any way.

HOW EARTHWORMS MOVE

An earthworm moves through the soil by expanding and contracting its muscles. To move forward, it pulls its body together at the front and relaxes it farther back, which stretches the back part of its body. As the earthworm moves through the ground, it feeds by taking in soil through its mouth and filtering out the nutrients that it needs before discarding the waste from its back end.

6 Watch the worm habitat over the next few days. Make notes about the effects of the worm's movements.

TIMELINE

	6000 BCE	300 CE
Atoms and Molecules	**2500 BCE** Tin ore is smelted in Turkey **4th century BCE** Greek philosopher Democritus believes the world is composed of tiny particles that cannot be divided	**1450** European metalworkers work out how to separate lead and silver ores
Electricity	**271 CE** The compass is first used in China; it works by detecting Earth's magnetic field	**1180** The first reference to the magnetic compass in Western writing is in Alexander Neckam's *Concerning Natural Things (De Naturis Rerum)*
Evolution		
Genetics		
Geology	**500 BCE** Xenophanes of Colphon (Greece) discovers that land can rise when he finds fossils of seashells on mountaintops	**1517** The Italian scientist Girolamo Fracastoro suggests that fossils are the remains of long-dead plants and animals
Gravity	**1450 BCE** Egyptians devise a water clock, based on the principle of dripping water **330 BCE** Aristotle believes that the Sun and planets orbit Earth	**1345** Dutch engineers use windmills to pump water out of areas that are being reclaimed from the sea
Light	**6000 BCE** People in Italy make mirrors from a rock called obsidian **1361 BCE** Chinese astronomers record a solar eclipse	**1021** Arab mathematician Alhazen writes about the refraction of light **1304** Theodoric of Freibourg, a German scientist, works out how rainbows form
Medicine	**2500 BCE** Chinese doctors begin using a pain-killing technique called acupuncture **1550 BCE** Egyptians are using about 700 drugs and medications	**365** Mechanical cranks are used to set broken bones in Greece **850** An Arab physician writes about eye disorders and treatments
Context	**c.3500 BCE** The wheel is invented in Mesopotamia **2630 BCE** Egyptians begin building the pyramids **776 BCE** The first Olympic Games are held in Greece **117 CE** Roman Empire reaches its greatest extent	**c.900** Mayan civilization in Mesoamerica collapses **1453** The Byzantine age comes to an end with the fall of Constantinople

1709 A model hot-air balloon is made in Brazil **1714** Gabriel Fahrenheit constructs a mercury thermometer	**1738** Daniel Bernoulli proposes a kinetic theory of gases **c.1787** French physicist Jacques Charles draws up Charles's Law of gas volumes	
1701 Edmond Halley draws up a map of Earth's magnetic field **1729** Stephen Gray explains electrical conductors and insulators	**1742** Benjamin Franklin demonstrates the electrical nature of lightning **1800** Alessandro Volta develops the voltaic pile electric battery	**1807** Humphry Davy uses electrolysis to isolate potassium and sodium **1822** André-Marie Ampere works out the laws of the movement of electricity
1650 Irish archbishop James Ussher mistakenly calculates that Earth was created in 4004 BCE		**1809** Lamarck wrongly states that characteristics acquired during life are inherited by offspring **1831–36** Charles Darwin on HMS *Beagle*
	1760s Robert Bakewell improves farmstock by selectively breeding animals	**1831** Robert Brown is the first scientist to describe a cell nucleus
1691 Naturalist John Ray believes fossils are ancient life-forms	**1793** Mammoth remains are found in Siberian permafrost	**1811** Schoolgirl Mary Anning discovers the first fossil ichthyosaur **1815** Eruption of Mount Tambora in Indonesia modifies climates worldwide
1609 Johannes Kepler draws up laws of planetary motion **c.1665** Isaac Newton formulates his law of gravity		
1665 Robert Hooke proposes that light travels in waves **1671** Isaac Newton shows that a prism splits light into a spectrum		**1811** William Wollaston invents the *camera lucida* **1839** Louis Daguerre invents a kind of photograph taken on metal plates
1628 Physician William Harvey explains the circulation of blood **1721** Smallpox inoculation is carried out in North America	**1745** The French surgeon Jacques Daviel successfully removes a cataract from a patient's eye—the first time this has happened	**1805** Japanese physician Seishu Hoanoka performs surgery with general anesthesia **1811** Charles Bell pioneers study of the nervous system
1630 English Puritans colonize Massachusetts Bay **1665** Bubonic plague kills one-fifth of London's population	**1787** The United States Constitution is adopted **1789** The French Revolution begins with the storming of the Bastille	**1803** The Louisiana Purchase doubles the size of the United States **1833** A law is passed in Britain to abolish slavery in the British Empire

1600 **1730** **1800** **1850**

TIMELINE

	1850	1900
Atoms and Molecules	**1892** James Dewar invents the vacuum bottle **1896** Henri Becquerel discovers radioactivity **1897** Physicist J.J. Thompson is the first person to identify electrons	**1905** Albert Einstein publishes his special theory of relativity **1910** The existence of the nucleus of an atom is proven by Ernest Rutherford
Electricity	**1877** American engineer Thomas Edison invents the phonograph **1885** American electrical engineer William Stanley makes the first transformer	**1923** John Logie Baird makes a type of television
Evolution	**1856** Male Neanderthal skeleton found; it differs in important ways from modern human skeletons **1859** Charles Darwin publishes *On the Origin of Species*, arguing his case for evolution	**1908** Marcellin Boule reconstructs a skeleton of a Neanderthal person **1938** A coelanth "living fossil" is found in the ocean off the South African coast
Genetics	**1865** Gregor Mendel, an Austrian monk, puts forward his laws of inheritance; these are published the following year	**1909** Danish botanist Wilhelm Johannsen defines a gene **1913** Chromosome mapping is pioneered by Alfred Sturtevant
Geology	**1861** The first fossil *Archaeopteryx* is found **1883** Mount Krakatoa, in Indonesia, erupts; it is one of the largest volcanic eruptions in recorded history	**1913** Earth's age is calculated at 4.6 billion years by geologist Arthur Holmes **1935** Richter scale proposed to measure earthquake intensity
Gravity	**1851** Léon Foucault builds a pendulum (Foucault's pendulum) that shows Earth's rotation. **1891** John Poynting, an English physicist, works out the value of the gravitational constant	**1927** Georges Lemaitre suggests the universe originated with a "big bang"
Light	**1877** Joseph Swan, an English physicist, develops the first electric light bulb **1882** Albert Michelson calculates the speed of light to within 0.02 percent of the correct value	**1905** Albert Einstein publishes his special theory of relativity **1935** Transparency film invented by American amateur photographers
Medicine	**1885** Louis Pasteur manufactures a rabies vaccine **1898** The cause of malaria, the protozoa *Plasmodium*, is discovered by physician Ronald Ross **1903** X-rays first used to treat cancerous tumors	**1929** Hormone estrogen first isolated **1934** Radio waves used to treat cancer **1943** Kidney dialysis machine built by Willem Kolff
Context	**1861–1865** American Civil War **1876** The Sioux Army of Sitting Bull defeats U.S. forces at the Battle of Little Bighorn **1897** The Klondike Gold Rush begins	**1901** Guglielmo Marconi makes the first transatlantic radio broadcast **1914–1918** World War I **1939–1945** World War II

1950	1990
1952 The first hydrogen bomb is exploded on an atoll in the central Pacific **1960** First optical identification of a quasar **1967** Domestic microwave ovens are sold in U.S.	**1994** American scientists discover a subatomic particle that they call the top quark **2004** A "supersolid" is discovered by American scientists—it flows through another material without friction
1961 The first silicon chips are manufactured **1962** The first national live TV broadcast, a speech by President Truman in San Francisco **1975** First commercial personal computers sold	**1990** Work begins on developing the World Wide Web **2007** American scientists create flexible batteries by weaving microscopic tubes of carbon into paper
1960 Remains of human ancestor *Homo habilis* discovered in Tanzania **1983** Fossils of a 16-million-year-old ancestor of humans are found by Meave Leakey in Africa	**1993** The oldest-known human ancestor, *Ardipithecus ramidus*, is discovered by Berkeley scientists **2003** Footprints of an upright-walking human, who was alive 350,000 years ago, are found in Italy
1953 The structure of DNA is discovered by Francis Crick and James Watson **1959** Down syndrome discovered to be caused by an extra chromosome	**1994** The first genetically modifed tomato is sold in the U.S. **1996** A sheep named Dolly is cloned in Edinburgh **1998** Human stem cells are grown in a laboratory **2000** Human genome is roughly mapped out
1977 Frozen body of a baby mammoth found in Siberian permafrost	**1996** Signs of microscopic life are found in a meteorite that originated from Mars **1997** Fossils of *Protarchaeopteryx*, a birdlike reptile, are found **2000** The fossil remains of a dinosaur's heart are found
1957 The first satellites, Sputnik 1 and Sputnik 2, are sent into orbit around Earth by the Soviet Union **1969** Astronauts Armstrong and Aldrin "bounce" on the Moon's surface, showing that gravity is less there	**1992** Scientists at the University of Pisa, Italy, make the most accurate calculation of the acceleration due to gravity
1955 Indian scientist Narinder Kapany invents optical fibers for carrying light long distances **1962** Light-emitting diode (LED) invented	**1998** Lasers are first used by American dentists for drilling teeth **2005** Flashes of light are discovered to create X-rays
1950 Link between smoking and lung cancer found **1958** Ultrasound scans are introduced to examine unborn babies **1967** The first successful heart transplant	**1983** The human immunodeficiency virus (HIV) is discovered **1987** The first heart-lung-liver transplant is carried out by a team of British surgeons **2000** Works begins on making the first artificial heart
1955–1975 Vietnam War **1968** Martin Luther King assassinated in Memphis **1969** Neil Armstrong and Buzz Aldrin are the first people to walk on the Moon's surface	**1989** Communist regimes across Europe collapse **1997** Diana, Princess of Wales, killed in a car accident in Paris **2001** Attack on the World Trade Center in New York **2008** Barack Obama elected first African-American president of U.S.

1950 1990 2010

KEY PEOPLE

Francis Crick (1916–2004)
Crick studied in London, before going to work at the Cavendish Laboratory in Cambridge, England. There he met fellow scientists James Watson, Rosalind Franklin (1920–1958), and Maurice Wilkins (1916–2004) and set about studying the structure of the DNA molecule. After discovering that it is arranged in two long, twisting "ladders" wound around each other, they published their findings in the scientific journal *Nature* in 1953. Along with Watson and Wilkins, Crick was awarded the Nobel Prize for physiology or medicine in 1962.

Georges Cuvier (1769–1832)
Cuvier was a pioneering French zoologist who spent much of his life comparing the anatomy of living animals and fossils. At the time, most people still believed that no animal had ever become extinct, but his discoveries were to convince many that wasn't the case. In 1796 he described his analysis of the skeletons of Indian and African elephants and mammoth fossils. Cuvier established, for the first time, that the three species were different, and that the mammoth was extinct. This and other discoveries were landmarks in the history of paleontology (the study of ancient life-forms). Although Cuvier had shown that animals could go extinct, he did not believe they could change their form over time, or evolve.

Charles Darwin (1809–1882)
Born in Shrewsbury, England, Darwin was the son and grandson of physicians. As a young man he was appointed the naturalist on HMS *Beagle*, a ship that embarked on an expedition of discovery between 1831–1836. During that time, Darwin's eyes were opened to the extraordinary variety of plant and animal life, and his views on evolution began to develop. It was only in 1858, however, that he and fellow scientist Alfred Russel Wallace jointly presented a paper on evolution to the Linnean Society in London. The following year, Darwin's book *On the Origin of Species by Means of Natural Selection* was published. It provoked a huge controversy—because some people said it went against the teachings of the Bible—but laid the foundations for modern views on animal and plant evolution. Darwin spent much of his later years studying the behavior of earthworms.

Richard Dawkins (born 1941)
Dawkins was born in Kenya, to British parents, and studied at Oxford University, England. His book *The Selfish Gene* explained his views on evolution, which differ from those of scientists such as Stephen Jay Gould. Dawkins teaches at the University of Berkeley and Oxford.

Stephen Jay Gould (1941–2001)
Gould was born and grew up in New York where, when he was five years old, his father took him to the American Museum of Natural History. The young Gould saw a reconstruction of the dinosaur *Tyrannosaurus rex* and was inspired to find out more about fossils. In later life, most of his detailed research was on land snails, but he applied his views on evolution to plants and animals generally. Gould's studies led him (with Niles Eldredge) to put forward the theory of punctuated equilibrium in 1972. They argued that organisms usually go long periods when they evolve little at all, and that evolution usually occurs in rapid bursts. Gould was a popular author of books about evolution, and he often appeared on TV programs.

Henry Huxley (1825–1895)
After giving strong support to Darwin's theory of evolution, Huxley became known as "Darwin's Bulldog." Huxley came from a relatively humble background, growing up in Middlesex, England.

He had little formal schooling and taught himself almost everything he knew. Remarkably, he went on to be one of the finest anatomists of the late 19th century. Among other things he studied the relationship between apes and humans. Then, after comparing the dinosaurs *Archaeopteryx* and *Compsognathus*, he came to believe that birds evolved from small meat-eating dinosaurs, a theory that is widely accepted today.

Jean Baptiste de Lamarck (1744–1829)

Lamarck's first career was as a soldier in the French army. However, after being injured during a war between France and Germany, he was forced to retire from active service. He developed an interest in botany and invertebrates and, in 1801, published *Système des Animaux sans Vertebres*, in which he defined important natural groups of invertebrates. These groups included echinoderms, arachnids, crustaceans, and annelids, which are still recognized by zoologists. He believed that environmental factors cause animals to change, and he also thought that animals and plants generally become more complex as a result of these changes. His ideas on evolution were later shown to be wrong by Darwin and others.

Charles Lyell (1797–1875)

Geologist Charles Lyell published *Principles of Geology* in several volumes between 1830 and 1833. These books were to revolutionize people's views on the processes that have shaped Earth. They also had a big influence on Darwin's ideas. Lyell traveled widely to look at rocks and the forces that shaped them. He concluded that we can understand how Earth has been changed over millions of years by looking at the impact of rivers, oceans, volcanoes, and earthquakes in the modern world. This idea became known as uniformitarianism and goes against another theory, catastrophism.

Thomas Malthus (1766–1834)

Born in Surrey, England, Malthus studied at Jesus College, Cambridge, and later became a priest at a rural church. Malthus believed that a constantly increasing human population overstretched food and other resources that were vital to eliminate poverty. He was not convinced that increased production or technological advances alone could improve the conditions of humankind.

Pythagoras (c.580–500 BCE)

Pythagoras is thought to have been born on the Greek island of Samos. He was a philosopher and founded a school of ideas called the Pythagoreans. He is best known for his contributions to math.

Alfred Russel Wallace (1823–1913)

Wallace was enthusiastic about natural history and as a young man traveled widely in the Amazon Basin and the Malay Archipelago. His observations of the geographical variation between animals inspired him to think more and more about evolution through natural selection. By 1858 he was convinced of the reality of evolution and sent an article outlining his theory to Charles Darwin. This was published, along with a description of Darwin's own theory, in the same year. Among his many other contributions to the natural sciences, Wallace was one of the first people to raise concerns over the environmental impact of human activity.

James Watson (born 1928)

Watson was born in Chicago, where he graduated in biology in 1947. He became convinced that the chemical structure of genes was of crucial importance to their biological role. After moving to Cambridge University, he teamed up with Francis Crick. Together they discovered the structure of DNA. Along with Crick and Maurice Wilkins he was awarded a Nobel Prize in 1962.

GLOSSARY

adapt When a species changes to suit its changing environment.

allele One form of a gene. The gene for eye color, for example, has alleles for both blue or brown eyes. The brown allele is dominant.

bacterium (plural bacteria) A tiny, simple microorganism made up of a single cell.

botany The study of plants.

cell A microscopic compartment that makes up part or the whole of an organism.

chromosomes Threadlike structures within cells that carry genes. They are made of DNA.

clone An exact copy of a living thing produced by nonsexual reproduction.

Darwinism The theory that species evolve by natural selection.

DNA (deoxyribonucleic acid) The chemical found inside the chromosomes in cells, which contains the instructions that control heredity.

dominance An allele is dominant if it masks the effect of another allele for the same gene.

ecology The study of the relationship between organisms and their environment.

evolution The process by which species of living things change, or adapt, in response to changes in their environment.

evolutionist A person who supports the theory of evolution.

extinction When all the individuals in a species die out, so none is left. The species is then said to be extinct.

fossil The remains or imprint of a once-living organism that is preserved in stone.

gene A section of DNA that carries the coded instructions for a particular trait in a living thing.

genetic engineering The techniques by which scientists alter the characteristics of living things by adding new genes to their DNA.

genetics The study of heredity and variation.

geology The study of rocks and minerals.

heredity The process of inheritance, through which living things pass on their characteristics to their offspring.

mass extinction When hundreds or thousands of species all die out in a short space of time, probably because of a major change in the environment.

mutation A change to an organisms's DNA that occurs during cell division and that might be passed on to offspring.

naturalist A person who studies animals, plants, and other living things.

natural selection The process through which living things that are particularly well suited to their environment are more likely to survive and breed, and so pass on their characteristics, than individuals that are less well suited to their surroundings. Natural selection acts on variation and mutation to produce evolution.

organism Any living thing, such as a plant, animal, bacteria, algae, or fungus.

paleontology The study of fossils.

population The total number of individuals in a species, or the total number in a group that is geographically separated from other groups of the species.

recessive An allele is recessive if its effect is masked by the effect of another, dominant allele of the same gene.

selective breeding The process through which plant and animal breeders produce new varieties of living things by selecting individuals with desirable characteristics to breed from.

species The world population of similar individuals that interbreed to produce fertile offspring.

variety A group of very closely related living things within a species.

FOR MORE INFORMATION

BOOKS

Adamson, Heather. *Charles Darwin and the Theory of Evolution*. Mankato, MN: Capstone, 2008.

Bright, Michael. *Diversity of Species*. Chicago, IL: Heinemann Library, 2009.

Gamlin, Linda. *DK Eyewitness Books: Evolution*. New York, NY: Dorling Kindersley, 2009.

Gibson, Terry R. *Natural Selection*. New York, NY: Chelsea House, 2009.

Lasky, Kathryn. *One Beetle Too Many: The Extraordinary Adventures of Charles Darwin*. Cambridge, MA: Candlewick Press, 2009.

Luongo, Charlotte. *Evolution*. Tarrytown, NY: Marshall Cavendish Benchmark, 2010.

Nardo, Don. *The Theory of Evolution: A History of Life on Earth*. Minneapolis, MN: Compass Point, 2010.

Raham, Gary. *Fossils*. New York, NY: Chelsea House, 2008.

Silverstein, Alvin. *Adaptation*. Minneapolis, MN: Twenty-First Century Books, 2008.

Waller, Sally. *Fossils*. Minneapolis, MN: Lerner, 2008.

Ward, Amanda. *Charles Darwin and the Beagle Adventure*. Dorking, England: Templar, 2009.

Winston, Robert. *Evolution Revolution*. New York, NY: Dorling Kindersley, 2009.

WEB SITES

Due to the changing nature of Internet links, Rosen Publishing has developed an online list of Web sites related to the subject of this book. This site is updated regularly. Please use this link to access this list:

http://www.rosenlinks.com/scipa/evol

INDEX